Gardener

Seeds of Flowers, Freedom and Faith

A Gift from a friend

Marcin Marczak

Dedication

Dad, it's been over 1704 days since I last saw you, thousands of kilometres have separated us. I want to say thank you. Thank you for the gift of life, for the friendship we've developed over the years, and for the countless hours spent discussing gardening principles.

Wishing you a very happy birthday.

Your son.

Marcin

Acknowledgements

Thank you for all your generous help: Grażyna Wołoszczuk, Divya Prasad, Danielle Sutherley, Lindsay Ambridge, Alex Smith, Duncan Austin, Krzysztof Harazinski, Szymon Zagórski, Arooomie, Dontha, Poops, Lucy Curtis-Prior, David Perry, Anke Schaffranek, Frederick Emereuwaonu, Md Amir Hossain

Scripture quotations taken from the NIV - New International Version and NLT - New Living Translation

Credits: Images generate using DALL-E

Contents

Reviews

This book hooks you in from start to finish, you will not want to put it down. Marcin takes you through the beautiful journey of how a story about a young farmer in communist Poland can be used as a reflection of us today. I believe that this book will change lives, with deep introspection, we too can become gardeners, plant seeds in our lives and watch them bloom. **Danielle Sutherley**

This book is immediately captivating.... we follow the intricate steps of care and patience required to nurture a flower from seed to bloom. Yet, as we do, the narrative subtly draws us into a reflection on our own lives – how we, too, sow seeds in our hearts...

There are many dimensions and ways to interpret this compelling book, with its characteristically stark and powerful illustrations. ...It ends with a challenge for each of us and invites a practical engagement to inspire curiosity and learning in our children.

At its core, however, 'The Gardener' is a profound story about God's unwavering love and faith in each of us. I hope you, too, will discover reflections of your own life within its pages, just as I did. **David Parry**

I really enjoyed reading the book. The book is like a text book, where we can learn about sowing and reaping. The book explains in simple language and very clearly about how each of our action is like a sower sowing a seed and each action has a fruit too. So a good seed has a good fruit and a bad seed definitely has a bad fruit. We can stop the bad fruit in our life by not sowing a bad seed.

The author has given examples as we keep reading the book and it shows with different situations where the good seed sown is and how he fruit would be. With its clear and easy to understand language, the understanding of the book stays in our heart and helps us naturally to put to action more good seeds. I have read the book atleast three times and have learnt more each time. Thank you for sowing into this book, dear author, and helping us to reap good fruits. **Divya Prasad**

The gardener is written in a way that will encourage all readers, young , old, not so old, to pause, step back and look at their thought life and behaviour.

The pictorial style and structure beautifully enhances this message. Showing that all things are possible to those who believe (Mark 9:23) **Lindsay Ambridge**

Chapter 1

Seeds of Flowers

They wanted to catch the 5 a.m. bus, but she fell off her bike onto a gravel road. They were both young and full of dreams in the early days of their marriage. They left their three little boys at home sleeping, hoping to return before they woke up, but it did not go as planned.

In the late 70s, Poland was slowly escaping the grip of a communist tyrant. After years of oppression, a revolution yearning for freedom swept the land, but it was brutally squashed, and blood flowed through the streets.

Yet, like a seed with a strong underground root system, hope persisted in people's hearts.

The communist regime oppressed the nation for several decades. Everyone was forced to submit to the master and follow the steps dictated by the ideas introduced by Karl Marx, desiring to create a society without any class and where no one owned any private property.

Entrepreneurship was viewed as an enemy of the state because it led to independence from the master.

Freedom was removed, and farmers were forced to produce out of small plots of land and give a portion of the produce to the slave master. If they missed their payment, the master would crack the whip and force them to obey.

The soil is designed to incubate and bring 30, 60, or even 100-fold return, so any farmer who understood the secret under his feet could become bigger and stronger.

However, when that happened and was reported, the slave master regime would immediately bring him down low, crack the whip, divide the land and, in some cases, even confiscate the property out of fear of the children multiplying and growing in strength.

Much like the ancient Egyptians who feared the growing strength of the Israelites, the government imposed strict limits on farm sizes, so anything above a certain level could not be exceeded; because it was perceived as a threat to the nation.

History likes to rhyme, just as in ancient times:

> "So the Egyptians made the Israelites their slaves. They appointed brutal slave drivers over

> them, hoping to wear them down with crushing labor. They forced them to build the cities of Pithom and Rameses as supply centers for the king. But the more the Egyptians oppressed them, the more the Israelites multiplied and spread, and the more alarmed the Egyptians became. So the Egyptians worked the people of Israel without mercy. They made their lives bitter, forcing them to mix mortar and make bricks and do all the work in the fields. They were ruthless in all their demands."
> Exodus 1:11-14 NLT

The wisest man who ever lived said, "There is nothing new under the sun."

Seeking a Better Future

Hoping for a different life, the gardener and his wife had tried many things before, including taking a five-day train trip back and forth to Vienna. They also travelled on a train to Turkey and Bulgaria, trying to buy leather jackets and jeans to resell at a profit. But that was too risky.

Behind the iron curtain, there were not many options available. However, they still had soil under the ground that was ready to multiply.

On that particular day, the gardener and his wife were on their way to the market to finally sell the produce of the land. They had been waiting patiently for that day for a long time. They believed what they found could be the answer to a better future, but instead of a great day, his wife was lying on the gravel road with flowers around her.

That year, the ground had produced bountifully. He carried eight packages, and she took six. Each pack had 30 flowers, so in total, there were 420 gladiola flowers between them both. They had no car, so they took bicycles to the bus stop, but they overestimated. A strong wind blew, and she lost her balance and fell.

As she was lying on the gravel road, all the questions started coming in:

> *What if it's the wrong direction?*
>
> *What if it doesn't work?*
>
> *Maybe she should have stayed home with the children.*
>
> *Maybe they should have followed the old path instead of venturing in a new direction.*

He helped her to get back up; thankfully, she wasn't hurt, and the flowers were not damaged.

They managed to catch a bus to the Warsaw flower market.

They sold everything they brought with them. On the way back home, it felt surreal. They had taken something from the ground and were returning home with real money.

The dream was real, and now they had proof that it worked.

The Beginning

The gardener grew up in a farmer's family, born three years after the Second World War finished. He loved planting ever since he was a child. His mother had told stories about him bringing home little trees from the forest and planting them around the house.

Since attending gardening school, he was exposed to new ideas, new ways of thinking, and new possibilities. He started to dream.

Fresh out of gardening school, he got a job in Wola Mrokowska budding roses.

One day he brought home a cigarette packet, filled with around 20 tiny bulbs of gladioli.

Full of excitement and expectation, he decided to try. If it worked out, it could change everything.

That was an important year; he was getting married the following year.

The first attempt was tiny. After planting all the seeds, the area covered was less than 1m by 1m.

He watered the seeds, nourished them, and waited.

He knew the land was faithful, and it would produce automatically. This profound truth, 'First the blade, then the ear, then the full corn in the ear,' mirrors the natural cycle of life itself

He knew how it worked and gained confidence in the process by observing his parents and grandparents harvest crops, following the same agricultural laws year after year without fail.

In the autumn, his new bride helped him dig all the bulbs from the ground. That year, he asked her to collect every seed, even the tiny ones, as small as black pepper. But he promised her they would not need to dig out the tiny ones from the following year onwards because he understood they would multiply and give enough for the coming seasons.

It was exciting; each bulb produced many baby seeds, some of them five and some even as many as ten.

They took the bulbs, put them into boxes, and waited for the following spring to come. They started dreaming.

> *What would it be like if all of the seeds produced flowers?*
>
> *What would it be like if they started reproducing and creating more baby seeds?*
>
> *What could be possible?*
>
> *Could this change their lives?*

New possibilities suddenly opened up, and the impossible started becoming possible. He knew he had to play his part and cooperate with the laws and seasons. Each of the four seasons has a very different purpose, so he had to discern and coordinate his actions with them.

He had hope in his heart; the vision was real. He held onto that picture. His heart was already believing. It was like becoming pregnant; giving birth was imminent.

> "Watch your thoughts; they become your words; watch your words, they become your actions; watch your actions, they become your habits; watch your habits, they become your character; watch your character, it becomes your destiny." Lao Tzu

Understanding the Harvest

A gardener needs both knowledge and discipline to achieve a successful harvest. He kept on reading books and improving the processes.

Timing is crucial, as flowers must be ready by a specific date, i.e. before Anka name day, which falls on the 26th of July. So they had to plant the bulbs before the 8th of April. However, they had to watch for frosty Zośka on the 15th of May, which could ruin the crops. Proverbs ruled the Polish gardening profession.

Most importantly, they had to be patient. Even though the ground produced faithfully, the cycle could only be repeated once a year. He had to see ahead to imagine and believe that as long as he kept planting the seeds, the earth would multiply them.

Many people saw the same opportunity and wanted the same results, but they got discouraged and gave up because the wait was too long.

> "...through faith and patience inherit what has been promised." Hebrews 6:12 NIV

Building a Family and a Business

They met at a holiday camp and after four years of dating, they got married on June 4th, 1977.

They lost their first child, a girl, and then they had three boys, fifteen months apart. His desire for a daughter led him to make one more attempt twenty years later. It was a boy again, so in total, four sons.

For the first six years of their marriage, they lived in two different places, forty kilometres apart.

It was challenging. Six months with her mother and six months with his parents, carrying three little children back and forth, along with furniture and even the flooring. They didn't have a car, so they had to ask neighbours to give them a lift every time they moved.

It was hard to juggle all the responsibilities — the little children growing up and the gardening business — but they had to do whatever it took to make the dream come to pass.

For the first five years, they had no other choice but to transport the flowers on bicycles.

Harvest

As the children grew, they were invited to participate in the gardening process, starting with preparing the ground, then raking, planting the bulbs, weeding, and eventually, the fun part, the harvest.

It was like a production line. The father cut the flowers with a sharp knife, watered by a purple denaturant. The boys carried the tall gladiolus on their shoulders to mum. The flowers were so tall that often they were taller than the little boys, who were 5, 6, and 7. The mum tied the flowers up with strings in bundles to be left overnight in a dark place, ready for the next day.

They had to wake up early to go to the market and sell the flowers. The demand for the flowers was so great at times that the moment they crossed the gates of the flower market, the car was immediately surrounded by ladies with trolleys, ready to buy it all out and resell it for more on the streets. They often snatched the flowers and outbid each other. It was fun to watch.

Then the autumn came and it was time to dig the bulbs out of the ground. They had a little transistor radio that operated without a cable. The latest technology powered the device using batteries so they could listen to 7 pm kids' evening stories as they dug out the bulbs from the ground. Happy memories.

Although they had to wait another nine months to plant the seeds again, the process was exciting and well worth the wait.

In addition to the flowers, the bulbs multiplied, allowing them to sell them as well, creating a second income stream.

The cycle was long, but now they could get paid twice a year, i.e. during Summer for flowers and in Winter for bulbs, which made things easier. He gained confidence; he knew he could repeat the process over and over again. The key was to be patient.

Here is to the power of consistency

After six years of repeating the process, the 20 little bulbs brought home in a cigarette packet in 1976 produced enough flowers and bulbs to finally replace the bicycles with their very first car in 1983.

He didn't have a driving licence yet, so the car had to wait, but he had good motivation to get it. The new car opened up possibilities, allowing them to increase both capacity and speed.

They continued the multiplication process. At its peak, they could sell as many as 15,000 bulbs in a single season and still have enough left over for themselves to plant.

At one point in the mid-80s, word about the flower farm got around and Japanese journalists visited the farm, documenting the plantation and publishing it in a Japanese newspaper. It was an exciting highlight.

グラジオラス

燃えたつ赤は祖国の血

After five more years of multiplication, in 1988, they started their next dream: building their own house, which they moved into in 1994.

Why this story?

You might ask: why did you choose to tell this part of the story?

I didn't.

I lived next to the gardener for 20 years and even carried the gladioli on my shoulders. I spent countless hours on the phone for another 20 years, sometimes discussing past memories, but I never knew this part of the story.

My eyes were not opened, and I never saw the memories arranged from this angle. It was like a ball of threads in different colours, yellow, green, orange, brown and black, all mingled together, which first needed to be untangled and cleaned before I could see.

I received the story during my morning prayer walk. I can take you to the specific place near the tree on a meadow where the picture of this book entered my heart. It came to me like a download from the internet, so I simply wrote it down.

Only after reading the Bible did I realise that the gardener used principles precisely described thousands of years ago. Even though the gardener didn't read it himself, he tapped into laws and principles passed down from generation to generation for millennia.

Chapter 2

Seeds of Life

How about you?

You might ask how that is relevant to me since I'm not a gardener.

Although this is the story of a man who loves gardening, it is not only his story. This is not an ordinary book; if you read it carefully, you could find your story inside this story.

If your heart recognises it, this book could be a junction.

This book is also a seed that could produce a mighty harvest.

The wisest man that has ever lived said, "There is nothing new under the sun".

We Are All Gardeners

The truth is, we are all gardeners. We constantly plant seeds, and we all bear fruit. Some of it is tasty, some not so much, so we also need to prune and sometimes even pull out the weeds. But it all always starts with a single seed. The principle of sowing and reaping is not just an agricultural concept but a universal law governing all aspects of life.

Have you ever wondered why everything that contains life within comes from a seed? Think about it, not only plants, animals, but even humans come from seeds.

As the book of Genesis reminds us, the process of sowing and reaping will never stop:

> "As long as the earth remains, there will be planting and harvest, cold and heat, summer and winter, day and night." Genesis 8:22 NLT

When was the last time you had a quiet moment, looked at the garden of your life, and admired the beautiful plants that have grown over the years and are now bearing fruit? You might have planted them with your partner, parents, or even grandparents.

Tasty harvests could be a great relationship, children, career, skill or investment.

Have you traced some of the tasty fruits all the way back to the day a seed entered the ground (heart)?

Do you remember when the seed was conceived and began to grow?

Looking back, your heart might be filled with gratitude for making such a good choice years ago.

On the other hand, you may have noticed some unwanted weeds in the garden that you might have tolerated way too long, and you know it is time to pull them out.

These weeds also started with a seed, and when you take a moment you will also be able to go back to that specific time when the weeds were conceived.

I grew up on a farm, attended a gardening school, and while at university I ran a gardening business. Though it was many years ago, I still love buying little indoor pots with seeds and watching them grow. They always bring incredible insight into virtually everything we do.

These days, the art of gardening seems so lost and foreign that when you ask a child where cucumbers come from, many of them answer confidently without blinking, "from the supermarket."....

Being detached from understanding the most important process built into virtually everything in our lives, hinders our ability to see things as a good gardener would, that is, with wisdom by looking at the longer perspective.

If we don't take time to reflect on what fruit our actions will produce, our vision is shortsighted, and that makes it hard to produce tasty fruit.

For this reason, I started buying and giving away pots with pre packaged seeds and soil as birthday gifts for kids and challenged them to find 15 Bible verses describing the growth process.

It's easy to think that things just happen to us, but that's not true, and it's not wise to look at life that way.

Recognising that everything always starts with a seed and is always followed by stages of growth, leads us to make better decisions.

So, how can we make better decisions?

King Solomon, considered the wisest man who ever lived, wrote the book of Proverbs about 3000 years ago. In the book he teaches us how to make better decisions.

The secret to better decisions is to start seeing things from a longer perspective, like a good gardener, who can see harvest by looking at seeds.

King Solomon mapped out for us different types of seeds and linked them to various types of harvests, so we can see the end from the beginning, and as a result we can make better decisions.

Here are just a few examples.

"Lazy hands (seed) make for poverty (harvest), but diligent hands (seed) bring wealth (harvest). Proverbs 10:4 NIV

A hot-tempered (seed) person stirs up conflict (harvest), but the one who is patient (seed) calms a quarrel (harvest)." Proverbs 15:18 NIV

"Pride (seed) goes before destruction (harvest), a haughty spirit (seed) before a fall (harvest)." Proverbs 16:18

"A generous person (seed) will prosper (harvest); whoever refreshes others (seed) will be refreshed (harvest): Proverbs 11:25 NIV

"The rich rule over the poor, and the borrower (seed) is slave (harvest) to the lender Proverbs 22:7 NIV Being a Slave (harvest) comes from borrowing (seed).

Using very graphic language, we could say it this way, if you make a lady called laziness pregnant, she will give birth to a child called poverty, and so on.

Remember, the fruit always reveals the seed.

The Book of Proverbs is a super short read—only about 30 pages long. It contains around 800 proverbs, teaching incredible wisdom by showing us the connections between seeds and harvest.

The Value of Wisdom in Life

It takes wisdom to see further into the future and recognise the rewards or consequences before they show up, or even by looking at the early stages of growth.

A young farmer learning from a more experienced one, eventually accumulates enough knowledge and understanding to be able to tell a harvest by looking at the first leaf of a plant or even a seed. Based on that, he decides if that plant needs to be pulled out or nurtured.

In a similar way a loving parent helps little children grow, by training them to see further, past the immediate gratification (playing games, eating sweets - seeds), and teaching them to engage in activities that will pay off in the long run (brushing teeth, cleaning their room, doing homework, saving - seeds).

In the same way, an experienced investor can tell which business is worth investing in and which is likely to fail. He can judge the future of a business with great accuracy by often examining the tiny leaves, which are the early stages of growing a seed.

A mature sailor refuses to get into a boat because of what looks to others like nice weather, but inexperienced youth often dearly pay for poor judgement and a lack of ability to see further. This is a skill worth developing.

Regardless, if you run a business or want to have a strong marriage, bring up children, be surrounded by beautiful relationships, enjoy strong mental health, grow a financial wealth, progress in your career or even enjoy a good physical health, all of these are gardens, where everything always starts with seeds and eventually produces harvest.

That's why gardening principles like preparation, planning, nurturing potential, choosing the right soil, pruning, patience or even entering a season of rest apply.

I encourage you to choose an area that matters to you most now, take a moment and think of specific people that you know of who have a beautiful garden in that particular area. When you reflect and ask yourself:

Why is their garden different from others?

What do you admire in their garden?

What plants are particularly beautiful?

What principles did they apply?

We all have areas where we need to grow. If you would like to become a better gardener, here are nine principles governing sowing and reaping.

Principle 1: A seed must be recognised

If you train your eyes to recognise seeds, you will start seeing them everywhere.

What are examples of seeds?

> Do you remember what started your career (harvest)? Was it because of a book (seed), inspiring conversation (seed), movie (seed)?
>
> Do you remember the first time you invested (seed) into something?

Do you remember the first time you borrowed money (seed)?

Do you remember your first beer (seed)?

Do you remember your first x-rated or horror movie (seed)?

Do you remember your first cigarette (seed)?

Do you remember when you stole something (seed)?

When I was around seven years old, we went fishing to Stara Warka with my father. After hours of not catching anything, I got bored and wandered off, and as I was walking along the river bank I found a net full of fish. Since no one was there, I took the net and brought it to my father hoping he would share my excitement. However, he was not happy and asked me to take it back. I told him that no one was there, but he insisted, so I had to do it.

He was happier with no catch and a bored child rather than making his child temporarily happy and allowing him to steal.

That was the moment when a weed was pulled out of my heart.

Another example of seeds is words; marketers understand this very well. They know that once their words (seed) create an image (conception) in our hearts after hearing them over and over, we become pregnant with the idea, and suddenly, we start desiring the product more and more, and eventually, we must have it, so we act on the desire.

Principle 2: A seed must conceive

How does a seed conceive? Have you ever thought about how a tiny seed starts the fascinating process of growth to eventually become a big plant that brings fruits with more seeds?

The Hebrew word for imagination is "Yetsa," which means conception. We literally get pregnant when we see ourselves participating through imagination.

When we plant a seed in the right environment, the heart is designed to bring a harvest automatically, regardless of what kind of seed we put inside, even if it means becoming an astronaut or Olympian, robbing a bank, or starting an affair. The soil (the heart) will produce by itself.

"I don't know how this happened to me" is not an entirely accurate description of a situation. It always starts with a seed and it always grows in stages.

Principle 3: A seed must be incubated

Have you ever considered why, despite constantly receiving loads of seeds (words, images), only a few of the seeds produce a harvest?

To answer this question, first we need to understand the incubation process.

Like plants, seeds need to be incubated, meaning they need to stay long enough in the right environment and be watered to grow.

There is a big difference between making a mistake once, and being pointed towards the right path vs being in an environment surrounded by people practising the same wrong behaviour, even laughing at the consequences and mocking any correction attempt.

In that kind of environment, there is very little hope for change, so if you ever find yourself stuck and want to grow a new seed, you might have to change the environment first.

There was a reason why God asked Abram to leave his father's house.

> "The Lord had said to Abram, "Go from your country, your people and your father's household to the land I will show you" Genesis 12:1 NIV

Principle 4: A seed must be watered to grow

Like in the natural world, for a seed to start growing, it must be watered.

How do we water seeds?

Do you remember a time when someone said nice words about you? Maybe it was a teacher or a friend. It could have been years or even decades ago, but you still remember and treasure the words in your heart. That's called watering the seed, thinking about it, imagining, reliving those moments in your heart.

This process was described two thousand years ago, when Mary watered the seed herself.

> "But Mary treasured up all these things and pondered them in her heart." Luke 2:19 NIV

The law of meditation, which involves holding an image of success until it produces a fruit, is also called visualisation. It is a well-known and common practice in sports psychology, business, and sales.

I met an Olympian once who could clearly describe a vivid picture she carried in her heart of participating in an Olympic ceremony before the big day.

The same process applies to meditating on something negative.

Maybe you remember when someone passed a careless judgement about you, or something you deeply care about, without knowing the whole picture, and it hurt you. As a result you kept returning to the conversation in your head and because you struggled to release that person in forgiveness you kept replaying it over and over in your mind.

Maybe you even argued with that person in your head, I know I have done it. That is also how a seed is watered and it grows.

I know of a man who lost a lot of money because of someone and for a long time, he could not forgive. He kept on meditating on the hurts until one day, the hurt was so unbearable that he decided to act on it, so he bought himself a gun and, with details, planned out how to kill the man.

He was in the final stages of growth; he even took regular trips around his house mapping it all out in his head how to bring the evil plan to pass. The fruit was ready for picking, thank God, at the last moment, he miscarried his very advanced and dangerous pregnancy. He forgave the man and got rid of the gun. He is alive and well today.

Both examples show how a seed grows by being watered through meditation.

Meditation means vividly imagining and reliving the experience over and over in your head, which keeps it alive. That's why forgiveness is so important.

Research shows that children spending time playing violent games are more likely to become aggressive and be involved in violence because they conceive and give birth to what they see.

The principle of reproducing what we look at, is beautifully explained in the story of Jacob. When working for his father-in-law Laban, Jacob utilised this principle to get paid for his hard work.

"Jacob, however, took fresh-cut branches from poplar, almond and plane trees and made white stripes on them by peeling the bark and exposing the white inner wood of the branches. Then he placed the peeled branches in all the watering troughs, so that they would be directly in front of the flocks when they came to drink. When the flocks were in heat and came to drink, they mated in front of the branches. And they bore young that were streaked or speckled or spotted." Genesis 30:37-39 NIV

So the flock gave birth to young that were streaked, speckled, and spotted because they were looking at fresh branches from poplar, almond, and plane trees with strips of bark peeled off making white streaks on them.

Everything is incubated in our hearts, so consciously choosing which seeds we allow into our hearts is extremely important. That is why wise parents help their children to learn how to make better choices and set healthy boundaries (movies, books, games, even friends).

Some people keep the trauma alive by revisiting the painful experience and telling others about it over and over again, so the seed stays alive and doesn't have the opportunity to heal and as a result the person is not able to move forward. Unforgiveness leads to internal torment (Matthew 18), i.e going back and forth in the mind replaying the conversation, arguing.

King David described a purifying process that takes place while reading the word of God; it removes pain, impurities, and trauma and heals the brain. King David said,

> "The Lord's promises are pure, like silver refined in a furnace, purified seven times over" Psalms 12:6 NLT

Principle 5: A seed must be protected from a miscarriage

Have you ever had a miscarriage? Do you remember a time when you had a dream that was so real that you could nearly hold it in your hands? You clearly knew there was a seed, even a blade, maybe even a head, but it didn't bring the harvest.

Why?

There could be a few reasons. Maybe somebody said something contrary to what you believed, or maybe you got distracted, and as a result you might have released the seed and caused the miscarriage, so we must protect our seeds from a potential miscarriage.

Principle 6: The earth produces automatically

The earth, the heart produces automatically

> "He also said, "This is what the kingdom of God is like. A man scatters seed on the ground. Night and day, whether he sleeps or gets up, the seed sprouts and grows, though he does not know how. All <u>by itself</u> the soil produces grain—first the stalk, then the head, then the full kernel in the head. As soon as the grain is ripe, he puts the sickle to it, because the harvest has come." Mark 4:26-29 NIV

"by itself" - The original Greek word used here is "automatos", and it means automatically, so the earth (heart) is designed to produce automatically. This is vital information, because the heart is created to grow seeds into plants.

Solomon teaches us in the book of Proverbs to

> "Above all else, guard your heart, for everything you do flows from it" Proverbs 4:23 NIV

Deciding what enters our hearts is on us, and it's extremely important because what is in our hearts influences everything we do.

Principle 7: The seed always grows in stages

Growth always happens in stages (blade, head, full grain in the head, harvest). As discussed above, nothing ever just happens to us. Every good gardener knows that the growth stages are part of the process and one stage will lead to another stage, so patience and wisdom are required.

> Hosea 8:7 shows "They sow the wind and reap the whirlwind..." NIV

For example, gossiping about a friend often leads to arguments and ultimately damages relationships.

Principle 8: The seed always produces according to its kind

> "Then God said, "Let the land produce vegetation: seed-bearing plants and trees on the land that bear fruit with seed in it, according to their various kinds." And it was so. Genesis 1:11 NIV

"according to their various kinds" - means potato seeds will only produce potatoes, sunflower seeds only produce sunflowers, anger will bring more anger, fear more fear and so on.

That's why we cannot fight evil with more evil, violence will only produce more violence. We need light to fight darkness, we need love to fight hate, we need forgiveness to fight unforgiveness because the seed will always produce according to its kind.

This was beautifully illustrated in the movie "GodFather" in part 3, when the main character Michael wanted to take the mafia money and start running an honest business but it didn't work out. There was always something invisible dragging him back to where he started, the seed produced according to its kind.

When planning for the next season's crops, every good gardener knows that choosing the right seeds is a very important decision. We must sit down, decide on the type of harvest we desire, then prepare the right type of seeds ahead of time, plant the seeds and be patient. If the gardener wants a good and specific harvest in the Autumn season, he cannot be careless with seeds in the Springtime.

Anything we want but do not have yet, is because we haven't planted the right seeds or maybe have not learned how to cooperate with the laws to bring up the fruit.

Anything that we do have but do not want to have, is very likely because we have not recognised the seed or stages of growth.

Principle 9: Seed's seed is in itself

"With seed in it" means every seed has a built-in design to reproduce perpetually. That's why God did not ever have to create another tree after the original creation because its seed was in itself, so it can reproduce forever.

That also explains the difficult question about the original sin: "Why has it been passed on to the human race?".

The answer is simple, because one type of seed cannot produce anything else; it will only reproduce according to its kind.

Understanding the law of sowing and reaping is essential to understanding other things. "Then Jesus said to them, "Don't you understand this parable? How then will you understand any parable?" Mark 4:13 NIV

Chapter 3

Seeds of Freedom

Who is the slavemaster?

In communist Poland, even though the farms produced bountifully, the shelves in the shops were empty. There was a shortage of everything, forcing people to wait long hours in front of grey buildings, with the hope of bringing home at least some of the most essential goods.

Fear, worry, hopelessness, and hardship were painted on people's faces. There were not many options available in the country behind the Iron Curtain.

After many long years, dissatisfied people (fertile soil) finally had enough and in the face of extreme adversity they began to whisper words of freedom (seeds).

The slave master failed to recognise it, until the seeds eventually developed a very strong underground root system.

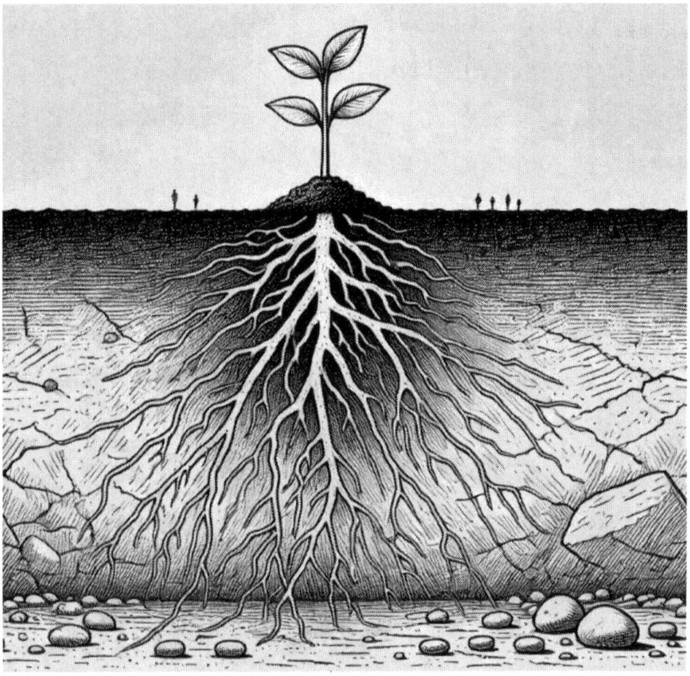

It was followed by rapid stages of growth, first the leaf, then the blade, until finally, the plant was far above the ground and visible to everyone.

No one could deny its existence.

It was obvious that in no time, the plant would bear fruit if not cut down.

The smell of harvest was already in the air.

The freedom song was no longer whispered behind closed doors; it was on the lips of many.

Enough was enough; the oppression could not be accepted any longer.

Like a new plant growing through the frozen ground after a long and severe winter, the change began despite the resistance.

Like a river that absorbed melted snow, demonstrations started flooding the streets, and the song of freedom was sung in the open.

Like a fire, infectious courage swept the land, awakening more and more people from their long winter sleep. People started joining the marches and singing the song of freedom, and eventually a revolution broke out.

In 1980, the Communist government imposed martial law in response to the growing influence of the Solidarity movement. Out of fear of children multiplying further and growing in strength, the government announced a state of emergency that lasted nearly two years.

Civil liberties, including travelling, were either taken away or severely restricted. The slave master tried to do whatever he could to kill the new plant, but it was far too late to abort the growing seed. They could not stop it anymore.

The plant bore fruit and the juices flowed to other branches. The tree was growing rapidly, bearing more and more fruit across the entire Eastern Europe, including Hungary, Czechoslovakia, Bulgaria, Romania and eventually even the Soviet Union.

Could this story ever be repeated?

We now live in a very different world, we have artificial intelligence, smartphones, and the internet. It is easy to think that a similar oppression and control from the government could never be possible again.

Is that really so?

Take a moment and ask yourself:

Is there a slave master?

Who is Pharaoh? And what is Egypt?

Has Pharaoh ever changed, or has he only changed his clothes?

If so, how can we recognise him?

When you take a moment and compare images from history next to each other, suddenly a new bigger picture emerges. Even though the images might come from different countries or even centuries, the fingerprints are identical.

Like a dark thread in a tapestry, his hand has been visible throughout history.

Like an uncomfortable acid reflux, he has been spewing fire, bringing division and killing baby seeds.

The tactics are the same. He has only changed his clothes. When you read the instruction manual, specific characteristics give his presence away.

> He wants to give you all the world's kingdoms if you only bow your knee and worship him. "All this I will give you," he said, "if you will bow down and worship me.." Matthew 4:9 NIV
>
> He is described as the "father of lies" or deceiver in John 8:44.
>
> He divides and hates unity. James 3:14-16

He disguises himself as an "angel of light", using religious or spiritual practices that appear promising but lead people away from the real living God. 2 Corinthians 11:14

He is prideful and ambitious and wants to be like the most high. "I will ascend above the tops of the clouds; I will make myself like the Most High" Isaiah 14:14 NIV

He uses fear as a tool to control and manipulate people to lead them away from their faith and trust in God. 2 Timothy 1:7

He seeks to steal, kill, and destroy, causing physical and emotional wounds. John 10:10

He tries to prevent seeds from taking root and bringing a harvest. "...Satan comes and takes away the word that was sown in them" Mark 4:15 NIV

He is an accuser; he brings condemnation, guilt, shame, and feelings of unworthiness. "accuses them before our God day and night" Revelation 12:10 NIV

When you take a moment you might see that the dark thread is visible all around us, even on a day-to-day basis at work, in business, in politics, or even sometimes in families.

Unfortunately many of the tools mentioned above have become part of the commonly accepted toolbox.

However, like a mechanic who lifts up a greasy spanner to get a job done, his hands eventually get covered in grease.

That's why it is so important to train ourselves to recognise fingerprints, as the seed will always reproduce according to its kind.

Division

During the communist days, the taskmaster, who hated unity, divided society into those who bent their knee and collaborated and those who did not.

If anyone chose to collaborate with the communist taskmaster, they had access to special shops and could buy virtually anything while others who refused to submit to the government suffered starvation.

It sounds like a passage from the Book of Revelation that describes a time in the future when, without the mark of the beast, you will not be able to buy or sell.

> "so that they could not buy or sell unless they had the mark, which is the name of the beast or the number of its name." Revelation 13:17 NIV

Solomon said there is nothing new under the Sun.

Chapter 4

Seeds of Faith

Tradition of men

I always thought there were many good books, and the Bible was one of them. We had a Bible somewhere in the house. When I was about five, I tried to read it but never got too far, so I gave up. I thought it must be for priests, not regular people like me.

I grew up with many traditions, but the Bible warns against the tradition of men,

> "Thus you nullify the word of God by your tradition that you have handed down." Mark 7:13 NIV

I had heard about God, and I even heard parts of the Bible read aloud during Sunday mass, but the Bible never came alive to me. The words didn't cut my heart. I didn't encounter the living God behind the words, so I didn't have a personal relationship with God.

Today I laugh that I had to go to a Muslim country to meet Jesus, because in Europe, God seemed to be hidden behind walls, complicated by religious institutions, distorted by hidden agendas of men and hidden behind many layers of traditions of men.

No one seemed to understand the Bible and God, unless you went to some kind of seminary. But even the people who attended seminary talked in such a way that simple people could not understand them.

How is that possible?

There is something wrong with this picture.

Jesus's disciples were simple people, fishermen, tax collectors, and even prostitutes.

He also said

> "...unless you change and become like little children, you will never enter the kingdom of heaven". Matthew 18:3 NIV

So it's not about the intellect but it's all about the heart.

Hulhumale Island

In September 2009 my wife and I took a leap of faith and left London for Asia.

On the beach of Hulhumale Island in the Maldives, I met a young man from Colorado. It was just after my 30th birthday.

In one of our casual conversations, he dared to say that the Bible is the word of God and he claimed it to be true. He was in his early 20s and I was around ten years older. In my heart, I arrogantly thought, I knew a thing or two more about life than he did. On top of that, I had met many religious people before and never really liked them.

When I tried to correct him, there was something different about him. He not only took a stand for what he believed, but he believed enough to take a bullet for it. He was willing to risk looking stupid, having someone potentially roll their eyes, or even laugh, but for some reason, he was ok with that.

Additionally, there was this amazing peace and lightness about him, which was very different from all the religious people I had met before.

For the first time in the 30 years of my life, I had come across someone who wholeheartedly believed.

I grew up in religion; I watched religion damage people by putting on them chains of guilt, shame, condemnation, or telling them they were never good enough.

Religion tells people what they need to do for God to be accepted by Him rather than helping them to understand what God has already done for them.

It might seem like a small difference in a sequence of words, but it is a massive difference in a relationship. It is a switch from do-to-be (do in order to be) to be-to-do (be in order to do). Switch from slave to son. Galatians 4:7

I always thought that God was somewhere in the sky, disconnected from people, often angry with me as I never measured up, and I felt unworthy even to try to talk to Him. But when I was reading the Bible, I saw something different.

God is love. 1 John 4:8, John 3:16 NIV

God is light; in Him there's no darkness at all. 1 John 1:5 NIV

He's a good God. Psalm 34:8, Psalm 100:5 NIV

He wants to have a personal relationship with me.

He met me in the Hulhumale apartment. That's where I had my first encounter. It was more powerful than anything I had experienced before. I was on the floor weeping. It was a flood of joy, peace and love going through my body like electricity.

Finally, the defences that I had built over the decades started coming down. His light was piercing through the walls of traditions of men that I had accumulated, as well as the stronghold of business self-development (religion without God) that I had turned to, to find answers to my broken life. It took 30 years, but my heart started to finally open up.

Now, I want to be the one who is willing to risk being laughed at.

Why?

Because it's worth it.

Forget religion as you might have known it.

As we set aside all the traditions that we grew up in, it is in the quiet space that we begin to hear the true voice of our heart.

He stands by the door of our hearts and knocks "Here I am! I stand at the door and knock. If anyone hears my voice and opens the door, I will come in and eat with that person, and they with me." Revelation 3:20 NIV

In summary, the Bible is about a rescue mission motivated by love.

> "The people walking in darkness have seen a great light; on those living in the land of deep darkness a light has dawned." Isaiah 9:2 NIV

All men were born into sin because of Adam and Eve's decision. It's easy to say it's unfair. As we discussed above, a seed can only reproduce according to its kind, so all men were reproduced according to the faulty seed of the original sin.

"for all have sinned and fall short of the glory of God" Romans 3:23 NIV

Every single person has sinned, regardless of their status, position. Every single person knows that in their heart. Regardless of how good a car they may drive or even how many charities they may have donated to, there is no difference. We all need a Saviour.

> "For the wages of sin is death, but the gift of God is eternal life in[a] Christ Jesus our Lord." Romans 6:23 NIV

But here's the good news:

> "But God demonstrates his own love for us in this: While we were still sinners, Christ died for us" Romans 5:8 NKJV

Jesus lived a sinless life and died for our sins. He made the payment for the sins for every single person on the planet, regardless of how good or bad they might have been.

Hope and salvation are available to everyone, so it's our personal choice to accept the gift of forgiveness and invite Him to live in our hearts. That is good news. That's why the gospel is often referred to as Good News.

Jesus is The Seed that gave birth to a new race of people. When you accept Him, you become born again.

> "Jesus replied, "Very truly I tell you, no one can see the kingdom of God unless they are born again." John 3:3 NIV

That's why

> "If you declare with your mouth, "Jesus is Lord," and believe in your heart that God raised him from the dead, you will be saved.." Romans 10:9 NIV

I have shared my heart with you, and now it is between you and God. God loves you - no matter who you are, no matter what your past is. God loves you so much that He gave His one and only begotten Son for you. The Bible tells us that

> "For God so loved the world that he gave his one and only Son, that whoever believes in him shall not perish but have eternal life." John 3:16 NIV

Jesus laid down His life and rose again, so that we could spend eternity with Him

Prayer of Salvation.

If this message touched you, if your heart recognises the truth, and if you would like to open your heart and invite Him in, I invite you to say this following prayer out loud and mean it in your heart:

> "Father God, I believe in You, Jesus I believe you died for my sins. I choose to turn away from sin, and I ask for forgiveness. Cleanse me and wash me clean. Father, I believe that Your son Jesus died on the cross to take away my sins. I also believe that He rose again from the dead so that I might be forgiven and made righteous through faith in Him. I invite you, Jesus, to come into my heart and be the King of my life. I choose to follow You and ask that You fill me with the power of the Holy Spirit. In Jesus' name, I pray.

If you said this prayer and meant it, you are born again. You are born from the new Seed and the Spirit of God lives on the inside of you.

> "If anyone acknowledges that Jesus is the Son of God, God lives in them and they in God." I John 4:15 NIV

I promise you, your life will never be the same. Even though you may still face challenges or even walk through the valley of the shadow of death, you will not walk alone. You have God almighty living in you. The Bible says He will never leave you nor forsake you: Hebrews 13:5

You are now a child of God. You have been transferred from the kingdom of darkness to the kingdom of light (Col 1:13), and now you have the Spirit of God inside of you. The exciting journey begins. It's time to discover who you truly are on the inside. Start by reading the book of John in the Bible.

I recommend connecting with other believers and finding a good church, but not one built on the tradition of men that nullifies the Word of God. Find a good, Biblebelieving church that will help you, sow into you and water you, so you can grow.

Start talking to God (prayer) and journal what He says to you. He invites us to abide in Him to bear fruit for His glory, John 15.

> "I am the vine; you are the branches. If you remain in me and I in you, you will bear much fruit; apart from me you can do nothing." John 15:5 NIV

God Himself is described as a Gardener.

> "I am the true vine, and my Father is the gardener." John 15:1 NIV .

If you said this prayer, please email me (below) and I'll send you a gift. I'm looking forward to hearing about your adventures with God.

Chapter 5

Seeds of Peace

Seed and a Fruit

This book is both a seed and a fruit. Writing this book was fun. As mentioned, I never planned to do anything like this. I simply didn't have any idea what to get my father for his birthday, so I went for a walk, spent time in prayer and wrote down what bubbled up in my heart.

I received this book in a similar way like downloading a file full of pictures from the internet.

When I tried to connect the images through my writing, I got stuck a few times.

The file was like a box filled with jigsaw puzzles designed for a 7 year old, given to a 5 year old.

But it had an invitation "let's do it together."

Instead of stressing out if it's possible to complete the book before the big day, I simply said, God, this was Your idea and You know how to complete it.

When I sat down to continue writing, trusting there is a way, suddenly all the puzzle pieces started coming together.

He never gives anything without an invitation to "Co create".

Since the birthday gift was to be in Polish, I was a bit concerned, I had not used my Polish writing skills for nearly two decades, but I was not alone. "Suddenly" I was reminded about some amazing people, including the parents of my friend from university with whom I had not spoken to for nearly a decade.

When I reached out, they agreed and generously gave countless hours reading through the manuscript multiple times and suggesting corrections. They are both retired teachers.

With the amazing help from so many people, within virtually six weeks or so I had the first version of the book in both English and Polish languages ready.

Finally, on September 11th I called my father.

The gift had arrived just in time, to be exact, that morning.

I asked him to unwrap the parcel.

He casually said, "ooh a book".

I said "look at the author".

He answered a bit more excited "Ohhh".

I said "look at the title".

He read “Gardener”.

I said: “That’s you dad, happy birthday”.

I asked him to make himself a coffee and sit down in an armchair.

I did the same in the UK. I took a sip of a coffee and started reading the book to him. It was a beautiful father-son moment that I will never forget.

An Invitation

As you are reading this book, you might recognise a gentle invitation to self reflection.

There might already be something bubbling up on the inside of your heart, please do not leave this precious moment and rush off to your next activity.

In today’s fast-paced world there's a tendency to constantly run to the next assignment, read the next book, watch the next video, listen to the next podcast...

However, that leaves people with forever collecting knowledge (seeds), but never taking the time to plant them. In today’s society there are many people with loads of facts (seeds) but not enough fruit.

Please recognise this special moment and give your heart a chance, your heart might be speaking to you with a very gentle voice. When that happens, I encourage you to take some time to journal.

Different Speeds of Our Hearts

It's important to realise that the heart has different speeds:

Listening speed - it is the fastest

Reading speed - it's in the middle gear

Writing speed - this is the slowest pace. When you pick up a pen and start writing or drawing, this is where the heart opens up like a flower and the new seeds with unlimited potential get a chance to start germinating, this is where the conception happens. Remember some treasures are hidden on the lowest shelves, so it's worth slowing down and reaching out for them.

The old art of handwriting seems to be gone and forgotten, but it does wonders to the heart as we slow down and start expressing what is on the inside.

How do we journal?

When Michelangelo was asked about his sculpting process, he answered: 'I saw the angel in the marble, and carved until I set him free'.

We journal in a similar way. Initially, your heart might only be able to recognise that there is something new. There might be just a feeling, an idea or even a sensation, but the mind might not yet have the right language to express it. That's ok. Stay with it until you will draw it all out.

It's important to remember, as with any skill, the more you do it the better you will become. It's a process that might require patience.

If you've never done it before, let's do it now.

Please take a piece of paper and recognise what's bubbling up on the inside of you and start looking for ways to express it by describing it more and more precisely.

Maybe you could start by putting down a single word on a page and create some simple branches, like a mind map.

Maybe draw an image.

Maybe start writing sentences down as they come, or

Maybe even dictate it to your phone.

Whatever works best for you, give it a go. At first you will very likely get loads of raw materials that might need refinement later on.

That's ok, let it all flow out of your heart. Grab them as they come and remain with it until you will draw it all out.

At the next stage, you will crystalline it more and more. As you stay with the process you will polish off the feelings into a clear picture and eventually you will 'set the angel free'.

For some, it might even feel like you are back in school during art classes, for some it might even feel childish, especially if your life requires you to operate daily using the logical side of the brain.

That's all right, stay with the process and rediscover the creator in you, we all have it.

As you are journaling, you are receiving seeds that are ready to germinate, seeds that could bring a mighty harvest in the years to come, it's worth investing time.

As you are expressing what is on the inside of you, ask yourself these questions:

> What is the picture?
>
> What baby steps could I take to start the journey in the new direction?

Albert Einstein is known for saying, "Imagination is more important than knowledge".

Cultivating Mental Health Garden:

By the way, there is a side benefit to this process.

The more time you spend doing the "heart work", the more you will realise how much healing it brings to your brain and your heart.

When you visit the secret quiet place, this beautiful calming process will bring soothing to your emotions, it will restore peace to your heart, repair and regrow new neural pathways in the brain. It does wonders. Fall in love with the process and watch your soul prosper.

In today's fast paced and overstimulated world, we need mental self care more than we realise, here are a few simple points to consider.

> Simplify life by reducing your plate. Do less but only the important things, this will help you avoid the trap of "piling up" that always leads to anxiety and stress.

> Reduce the signals - remove all possible notifications, and any application that has a "wall" (newsfeed) - trust me, you cannot beat the artificial intelligence and algorithm designed to get you to click, scroll and stay. They know all your "hot buttons" based on your browsing history. Social media "Walls" will quietly rob your inner peace and always lead to anxiety.

Set boundaries to protect peace, boundaries related to people, technology, type of information you allow in your life etc - peace is a currency that not enough people value enough to be able to pick it up.

Invest in and cultivate good relationships based around healthy principles like: love, contribution, generosity, pure heart, honour and joy. Ideally three different ones,

Someone at your level (Jonathan) - good friend

Someone above you (Paul) - mentor, to give you hope and a direction

Someone below you (Timothy) - someone you can teach & mentor, by contributing your soul will enjoy fullfilment

Be quick to forgive, do not harbour unforgiveness as we have learnt it is a fast growing seed, this is always a fast way to enter mental torment.

Increase the quiet time in order to connect your soul (thoughts, emotions and imagination) to life giving activities such as journaling, writing, reflecting, creating, planning.

Follow these simple principles and watch your mental health garden prosper.

For a moment, let's imagine the opposite in order to contrast the above picture: fill up your calendar with as many activities as you can. Do not leave breaks in between, run from one activity to another, pile up responsibilities and deadlines. Keep all possible applications and notifications turned on, keep refreshing "walls". Do not find time for relationships, be alone most of the time, and if you hang out with people, be around those who constantly cross boundaries and cause wounds, that will give you an opportunity to dwell on the hurts... you get the point.... Healthy boundaries are essential. The power to choose what plants will grow in our gardens is still in our hands.

Recognise the Two Voices

When journaling, it's helpful to recognise which type of the two voices you are hearing.

Is it a vision voice? or a correction voice?

Both of them communicate different but important signals.

Vision voice - It could be an inspiration leading to dreaming, hoping and believing for a bigger picture for you, or for your family, your community.

Correction voice - It usually is somehow an uncomfortable feeling but it's important to emphasise that it's not a feeling of guilt, it's not shame, it's not condemnation, it's also not a feeling of regret, as dwelling in any of the above rooms would be a dead end to the creative process.

In contrast, the correction voice is a gentle and loving course correction signal inviting you to a higher place and to raising standards in order to grow and to serve others. Usually required before a next assignment or preventing a roadblock ahead.

However, because this voice could be a bit uncomfortable, it is very tempting to immediately throw the "hot potato out". But please get curious and stay with it, especially if you are currently going through a crisis.

Purifying Gold By Fire

When walking through a fire, I invite you to journal the impurities that come up to the surface as this is how gold gets purified.

If you are not familiar with the process of gold purification, it's fascinating how it mirrors the character building.

Raw gold is heated up to extreme temperatures in order to melt it and cause the gold to separate from impurities. As the gold melts, all the dross rises to the surface (this could be anger, irritation, character flaws etc).

As they come up to the top, they get skimmed off leaving the gold in a more refined state. The process is often repeated multiple times in order to remove more and more of the impurities and make the gold purer with every repetition. The final result is malleable and transparent gold (teachable, humble and pure heart with an uncompromising character).

That's why journaling is so important, because reflection and writing it down is the "skimming off" part of the process.

If we don't capture the impurities, very likely we will get reheated to the extreme temperature again and again until we learn the lesson. This is never fun, but essential before any promotion or to guide us out of recurrent painful life events.

There are people who virtually never take time to self-reflect, they do not pause, to do an "after action review". They are not open for any correction, suggestion and as a result they keep learning the same lesson over and over. This is a very painful and dangerous way to live a life for the person who gets reheated and people around him.

"Godly sorrow brings repentance that leads to salvation and leaves no regret, but worldly sorrow brings death." 2 Corinthians 7:10 NIV The word repentance, that was used in the original Greek is "metanoia" and it means change of mind. Changing the way we think in order to eventually change the direction of our lives.

It pays off to train our heart to recognise the voice of correction, and write it all down.

A single course correction idea in the quiet moment could possibly dismantle a long destructive pattern or help us to avoid consequences in the coming future.

New Habit

If you don't have a notebook handy, I have prepared a few extra pages in this book and left a few prompts to help you to kickstart this process, so you could possibly start planting the first few seeds.

To cultivate reflection and grow in the intimate skill, I encourage you to develop it as a habit. Get yourself a good hardcover journal, find a quiet spot, have your dreaming chair, get yourself your favourite beverage, play some soft instrumental music, leave your phone in a different room or put it in airplane mode and start journaling. Remember, through intimacy, you will conceive and this is where you get to know God's voice, learn to abide and co-create with Him.

Wisdom

When you write down the first sentence in your journal, you will be surprised to know that there are other sentences, pictures and thoughts still available on any given topic and could be expressed if only they got an opportunity.

However, in the normal rhythm of life, such as talking, watching, scrolling, or even reading, these thoughts often do not get a chance to "say a word".

They are like a quiet friend who is in the room in the company of others, who will not speak over other people and refuses to shout to be heard.

This friend needs to be invited to speak, so when we stop to journal, we invite his opinion, we want to hear his voice and this is when the flow of wisdom begins. You will be surprised how much untapped insight there is available when only given a chance.

Seven Characteristics of Wisdom

To help you recognise if you are hearing the right voice, here are 7 characteristics to judge against:

> "But the wisdom from above is first of all pure (1). It is also peace loving (2), gentle at all times (3), and willing to yield to others (4). It is full of mercy and the fruit of good deeds (5). It shows no favoritism (6) and is always sincere (7)." James 3:17 NLT

The voice of God is never a voice of pressure, control, competition, pride, condemnation, guilt or shame, but a voice of a loving Parent inviting you to a higher place in order to help you get to know Him more, grow into who you always meant to be, and to serve others.

Hidden Treasures of the Secret Place

When you find yourself abiding in the secret place, this is where amazing solutions come, inventions are birthed, new businesses come to life, books are received, scripts for movies are downloaded, new music and songs are heard, new ideas bubble up for your family, communities or even nations. Possibilities are endless.

In the quiet place you will receive divine blueprints.

Noah received a blueprint for his ark, David received a blueprint for the temple, Moses received a blueprint for the tabernacle and so on.

I believe there are divine blueprints available for new healthcare solutions, gaming industry, sport, education, mental health, travel, government, entrepreneurship and so on. All based on the Kingdom principles such as love, care, relationships, generosity, transformation, longevity rather than a quick gain, cold transaction, squeezed profit or optimised conversions at the expense of people. There are new heights available, new standards, new strategies, witty inventions for those willing to dwell in the secret place and cultivate intimacy.

"Yes, I am the vine; you are the branches. Those who remain in me, and I in them, will produce much fruit. For apart from me you can do nothing."John 15:5 NLT

Hidden Themes

I encourage you to read this book more than once, as there are hidden themes that may only become visible on the second, third or even fourth reading.

Remember, timing plays a big part in planting. Seeds love fresh and well watered Spring soil, rather than frozen Winter ground.

Solomon said:

> "There is a time for everything, and a season for every activity under the heavens: a time to be born and a time to die, a time to plant and a time to uproot". Ecclesiastes 3:1-2 NIV

Chapter 6

Seeds of Action

Before we part, let's plant a few possible seeds.

Imagine a world where children at school would receive a pot with soil and seeds.

After planting and watering them, they would be asked to watch the growth of a tiny seed into seedlings, to budding, to flowering and eventually to fruit with seeds in itself.

Based on the observation they would be asked to write an essay on how they could possibly apply the same principles in their own lives to change the world around them.

What could they learn through the process?

What questions would they ask?

What would they imagine to be possible?

What new seeds would they plant in their gardens?

What new world would they create?

Flower Pot Challenge

If the gardener's journey inspires you, here is an exercise to put these lessons into practice. Please plant some physical seeds into a pot, and while watching them grow find fifteen Bible verses describing the process. Please email the picture of the plant and the verses to info@gardenerbook.com and I will send you a small gift and your next challenge.

Also consider giving children a similar challenge and watch them grow in wisdom. Simply search online for e.g "ready to plant pot with seeds and soil", this should make an interesting gift and a memorable bonding experience.

We are all gardeners.

> "As long as the earth remains, there will be planting and harvest, cold and heat, summer and winter, day and night" Genesis 8:22 NLT

Pay it forward

Most likely you have received this book as a gift from a friend.

This book is a fruit but it is also a seed. If you feel that reading this book brought you closer to planting a new seed in your own garden, please consider gifting this book to someone who could also find it helpful to learn these principles.

Please take a moment and think of a person who is currently going through a season in life, where they could benefit from planting a new seed in order to enter into a new season.

This could be related to growing gardens of healthier relationships, better finances, stronger mental or even physical health.

Or maybe you simply know of someone who loves gardening at the heart and could enjoy reading this book.

Let this book continue being a gift from one friend to another.

Together we could plant a few trees that bear good tasty fruit and make this world a little bit of a better place.

Remember "The best time to plant a tree was 20 years ago. The second best time is now."

Whatever you are going through currently, or whatever has already happened, I encourage you to take this moment and plant something new regardless of the past missed opportunities.

Let the new plant bring joy to your heart as you watch it grow.

Review

Also, if you enjoyed this book, please consider leaving a review on Amazon to help us reach more gardeners. Thank you for reading and I wish you happy and fruitful planting.

www.gardenerbook.com info@gardenerbook.com

Capture seeds as they come.

Gardens (spiritual, physical health, mental, relationship, financial etc)

Through intimacy, you conceive. Stay with it.

What's the picture?

'I saw the angel in the marble, and carved until I set him free'. Michelangelo

What baby steps can you take to move towards the picture today?

Printed in Great Britain
by Amazon

55291041R00053